Sovereignty and Authority in the Context of the American Republic— A Confessional Lutheran Assessment

Sovereignty and Authority in the Context of the American Republic— A Confessional Lutheran Assessment

Rt. Rev. James D. Heiser, M.Div. S.T.M.
Bishop of the Evangelical Lutheran Diocese of North America

REPRISTINATION PRESS
MALONE, TEXAS

REPRISTINATION PRESS
716 HCR 3424 E
MALONE, TEXAS 76660

www.repristinationpress.com

ISBN-13: 978-1891469572
ISBN-10: 1-891469-57-6

Preface.

Given the fact that a quite voluminous body of literature has been generated on the broad topic of the 'Church-State' relationship in the theology of Martin Luther, the brevity of the following essay may, all on its own, be an offense to some readers. However, this brevity is not the result of a lack of awareness of that literature—far from it. Since the author first began researching this topic in 1989, he has become painfully aware of the sheer quantity of such work. However, the purpose of this essay is not a tedious recapitulation of the entirety of the germane literature; rather, the intention is two-fold: first, to summarize the change which occurred in the mature theology of Luther, and to offer a brief reflection on the impact this had throughout the Age of Lutheran Orthodoxy, and thus the way in which the Pietists perverted Lutheran teaching and practice regarding this article of faith; second, the implications of Luther's mature understanding of the relationship between the Christian and Caesar are applied to the American Republic.

The author has few illusions regarding the general public indifference both with regards to Lutheran theology and to the political philosophy of the founding fathers of the American Republic. Some readers may question the significance and practical application of such reflections as are offered in the following pages, given the low esteem in which both doctrinal and constitutional original intent are held in these latter days. However, it is our intent in these few pages simply to illumine several dark corners in the history of the complex topic of the relationship between the Christian and civil authority.

+*James D. Heiser*
Bishop, The Evangelical Lutheran Diocese of North America
Malone, Texas

The demonic trend in political thought makes its appearance at the very point which we designate as the birthday of the modern times.

Bp. Eivind Berggrav[1]

Introduction.

Conventional wisdom holds that two of the topics forbidden to polite discussion are religion and politics. Since these are two domains concerning which thinking human beings must necessarily form views to bring a degree of cogency to their overall worldview, the opprobrium of Demos in response to such ruminations is all the more frustrating. However, such opprobrium is perhaps comprehensible given the degraded condition of much of the theologico-political discussion in the public square of the American Republic.

Attempts by adherents of the Unaltered Augsburg Confession to speak within our dogmatic tradition to the thornier concerns of the body politic have often been flawed by a distorted understanding of that tradition. This distortion started in Pietist circles which promoted Quietism in support of Prussian Absolutism, and was further expanded by both apologists for, and opponents of, Nazi Germany. The result has been that the legacy of Martin Luther and his noble coadjutors of the Lutheran Reformation has been posthumously altered to such a point that the understanding of the three estates which was enunciated in the later days of the Reformation has been almost completely lost. Just as the mature theology of Martin Luther concerning Church and Office has often been distorted by an overemphasis on his early writings (e.g. the infamous "three books" of 1520: *To the Christian Nobility of the German*

---

1   Eivind Berggrav, *Man and State*, trans. by George Aus, (Philadelphia: Muhlenberg Press, 1951) p. 5.

Nation, The Babylonian Captivity of The Church, and *On the Freedom of a Christian*), the "Lutheran" understanding of the State has been reduced to his *A Sincere Admonition (1522) Temporal Authority (1523),* and *Against the Robbing Murdering Hordes of Peasants* (1524).[2] After generations contending with the distorted view of Luther's doctrine of the ministry presented by those Lutheran theologians who seem unaware of any Lutheran writings after 1529,[3] arriving at a correct understanding of the State requires an examination of the teaching of the Lutheran theologians and jurists after the Diet of Augsburg of 1530—especially in the context of the Smalcald League's concerns regarding the possibility of an imminent attack by the forces answerable to Emperor Charles V.

Writing for *The Sixteenth Century Journal* in 1972, Eric Gritsch observed that "A survey of the literature on Luther's attitude toward political order and disorder reveals not only the neuralgia, but also the nostalgia and even paranoia that are rampant in the many camps of Luther interpreters."[4] The past four decades have added little clarity in this regard, as the woefully inadequate state of Luther studies has continued and even exacerbated the situation described by Gritsch.

The scope of the present study is necessarily relatively narrow, focusing on the relationship of sovereignty and authority, examining Luther's early and mature views on this topic as a means for examining the received self-understanding of the American Republic.

---

2   There were, of course, other treatises which deal in whole or in part with matters which pertain to the secular authorities. However, these three works are highlighted because of their parallel significance to the 1520 treatises in the awareness of most modern Lutherans.

3   What other plausible reason could be offered to explain why men who purport to be Lutheran pastors and theologians are unaware of the fact that the Apology of the Augsburg Confession grants that ordination may be considered a sacrament (AP Art. XIII:10)?

4   Eric W. Gritsch, "Martin Luther and Violence: A reappraisal of a Neuralgic Theme," *The Sixteenth Century Journal,* vol. 3, no. 1 (Apr. 1972), p. 40.

Martin Luther—From the Peasants' War to the Smalcald League.

The views of the 'early Luther' as they pertain to the authority of the State emerge in the midst of the theological and political chaos which began with the 'reforms' undertaken in Wittenberg by Andreas Karlstadt (1486–1541) during Luther's seclusion in the Wartburg (May 1521–March 1522) and culminating with the Peasants War of 1525 and exacerbated by Thomas Müntzer (1489–1525).

The chaos which Karlstadt unleashed in Wittenberg was part of a rising discontent which Luther detected during a trip from the Wartburg back to Wittenberg in December 1521 in his disguise as "Junker Georg." Upon his return to the Wartburg, Luther penned a work which was published in March 1522 with the title, *A Sincere Admonition by Martin Luther to All Christians to Guard Against Insurrection and Rebellion.*[5] In this work, Luther observed that "the pope and his anti-Christian regime shall be destroyed," but that "the papacy and the clerical estate will not be destroyed by the hand of men, or by insurrection."[6] Although he maintained that "the wickedness [of the papacy] is so horrible that no punishment is adequate except the wrath of God itself," Luther left the suppression of that wickedness "to the temporal authorities and nobility. They should, of course, take action, each prince and lord in his own territory, by virtue of the obligations incumbent upon such duly constituted authority; for what is done by duly constituted authority cannot be regarded as insurrection."[7] As far as the 'common man' was concerned, Luther counseled caution: "But we must calm the mind of the common man, and

---

5   for a modern translation, see *Luther's Works*, vol. 45 (Philadelphia: Fortress Press, 1962), p. 57–74. (Hereafter AE 45.)
6   ibid., p. 60–61.
7   ibid., p. 61.

tell him to abstain from the words and even the passions which lead to insurrection, and to do nothing in the matter apart from the command of his superiors or an action of the authorities."[8] In support of this proposition, Luther offered the following reasoning:

> First, as has been said, the threats of violence will not be implemented. All that men are saying and thinking on the subject is nothing but idle chatter and vain imaginings. ...

> Second, even if insurrection were a practical possibility, and God were willing to impose so merciful a punishment upon them, it is still an unprofitable method of procedure. It never brings about the desired improvement. For insurrection lacks discernment; it generally harms the innocent more than the guilty. Hence, no insurrection is ever right, no matter how right the cause it seeks to promote. It always results in more damage than improvement, and verifies the saying, "Things go from bad to worse." ...

> Third, God has forbidden insurrection, where he speaks through Moses, "*Quod iustum est, iuste exequaris;* Thou shalt follow justly after that which is just," and again, "Revenge is mine; I will repay." ...

> Fourth, in this particular case, insurrection is most certainly a suggestion of the devil. ... Now he is at work trying to stir up an insurrection through those who glory in the gospel, hoping thereby to revile our teaching as if it came from the devil and not from God.[9]

One perceives that at this point, the emphasis of Luther's admonition is eminently practical,[10] although he does not exclude a theological component.

8   ibid., p. 62.

9   ibid., p. 62–64.

10   The first two points essentially reduce to, 'it won't happen' and 'it wouldn't work anyway'.

When he considered the possibility that the authorities would fail to reform the Church, Luther made it clear that it is *not* that the public is to remain idle; rather, "First, you are to acknowledge your own sins, because of which the strict justice of God has plagued you with this anti-Christian regime". Luther then admonished the people to "in all humility pray against the papal regime" and "let your mouth become such a mouth of the Spirit of Christ as St. Paul speaks of in the text quoted above, 'Our Lord Jesus will slay him with the mouth of his Spirit.'"[11] Again, Luther's appeal was largely practical, based in the notion that an insurrection raised against papal tyranny will not 'work': "He can be handled better this way than with a hundred insurrections. By resorting to violence we will do him no harm at all, but rather strengthen him, as many have experienced before."[12] Thus, Luther concluded, "there is no *need* for you to demand an armed insurrection. Christ himself has already begun an insurrection with his mouth, one which will be more than the pope can bear."[13] In his conclusion, Luther freighted his argument as "a renewed admonition to guard against insurrection and giving offense, so that we ourselves may not be agents for the desecration of God's holy word."[14] At this point, Luther appears to have believed that the collapse of papal power was inevitable; he wanted there to be no confusion as to the nature of the pope's downfall. Insurrection, he believed, would not only be wrong—it would be inexpedient.

Luther's next significant treatise on the topic was his 1523 work, *Temporal Authority: To What Extent it Should be Obeyed*. An extensive analysis of this work falls outside the scope of this brief essay, but a few observations are in order as pertains to Luther's hardening views regarding insurrection. Luther's view at this point is that, "we must divide the children of Adam and all mankind into two classes, the first belonging to the kingdom of God, the second to the kingdom of the

11   ibid. p. 66–67.
12   ibid. p. 67.
13   ibid., p. 67–68. Emphasis added.
14   ibid., p. 74.

world."[15] As far as the Christians were concerned, there was no need for temporal government: "Now observe, these people need no temporal law or sword. If all the world were composed of real Christians, that is, true believers, there would be no need for or benefits from prince, king, lord, sword, or law."[16] If such words are stripped of their context, it is not hard to see that Luther can be misquoted to accomplish a great deal of mischief. Indeed, it would be such assertions—stripped of their context—that would become a source of great trouble throughout the mid-1520s, for there were plenty of fanatics ready to imagine establishing such a world. But Luther went on to declare:

> If anyone attempted to rule the world by the gospel and to abolish all temporal law and sword on the plea that all are baptized and Christian, and that, according to the gospel, there shall be among them no law or sword—or need for either—pray tell me, friend, what would he be doing? He would be loosing the ropes and chains of the savage wild beasts and letting them bite and mangle everyone, meanwhile insisting that they were harmless, tame, and gentle creatures; but I would have the proof in my wounds. Just so would the wicked under the name of Christian abuse evangelical freedom, carry on their rascality, and insist that they were Christians subject neither to law nor sword, as some are already raving and ranting.[17]

Luther urged Christians to take an active role in the governance of the "kingdom of the world": "Therefore, if you see that there is a lack of hangmen, constables, judges, lords, or princes, and you find that you are qualified, you should offer your services and seek the position, that

---

15   AE 45:88. Such a distinction is, of course, hardly unusual in the theology of the Western Church: St. Augustine's *de civitate Dei* is predicated on this distinction, and that work proved instrumental in shaping the entire doctrine of history in Western Christendom for nearly a thousand years.

16   AE 45:89.

17   AE 45:91.

the essential governmental authority may not be despised and become
enfeebled or perish. The world cannot and dare not dispense with it."[18]
In short, Luther was neither a Utopian nor a 'Quietist': Christians are
obliged to embrace vocations which are expressed in the full range of life
set forth in the Small Catechism's Table of Duties.

The vital thing for the Christian to remember is that there is a
strict limit on the authority of such worldly powers: "The temporal government has laws which extend no further than to life and property and
external affairs on earth, for God cannot and will not permit anyone but
himself to rule over the soul. Therefore, where the temporal authority
presumes to prescribe laws for the soul, it encroaches upon God's government and only misleads souls and destroys them."[19] Indeed, even at
this early date, Luther was beginning to comprehend that there would
be occasions when worldly authority must be resisted:

> If your prince or temporal ruler commands you to side with the
> pope, to believe thus and so, or to get rid of certain books, you
> should say, "It is not fitting that Lucifer should sit at the side of
> God. Gracious sir, I owe you obedience in body and property;
> command me within the limits of your authority on earth, and
> I will obey. But if you command me to believe or to get rid of
> certain books, I will not obey; for then you are a tyrant and
> overreach yourself, commanding where you have neither the
> right nor the authority," etc. Should he seize your property on
> account of this and punish such disobedience, then blessed are
> you; thank God that you are worthy to suffer for the sake of the
> divine word. Let him rage, fool that he is; he will meet his judge.
> For I tell you, if you fail to withstand him, if you give in to him
> and let him take away your faith and your books, you have truly
> denied God.[20]

---

18   AE 45:95
19   AE 45:105
20   AE 45:111-112.

Rightly understood, this is a quite striking assertion. Anyone who would reduce even the early Luther to simply defending 'freedom of conscience'—while remaining passive in the face of tyranny—fails to grasp the import of what is being asserted here. Although the "prince" may have certain authority over "body and property," that authority ceases where it intersects the free exercise of the faith; the defense of the free exercise of faith extends to at least a noncompliance with unjust attempts to seize possessions (whether such possessions belong to the church, or to individual Christians) which relate to the exercise of the faith. The Christian is bound to uphold those matters pertaining to the faith, even if it means defying the prince. Furthermore, Luther maintained that the prince had no business bringing force against those who believe false doctrine: "Heresy can never be restrained by force. ... Here God's word must do the fighting. If it does not succeed, certainly the temporal power will not succeed either, even if it were to drench the world in blood."[21]

Furthermore, in the third portion of *Temporal Authority*, Luther makes it clear that citizens are not bound to fight for the secular authority when they know that the prince's cause is unjust. In the case of a just war, "subjects are in duty bound to follow, and to devote their life and property, for in such a case one must risk his good and himself for the sake of others." But then Luther asked:

> What if a prince is in the wrong? Are his people bound to follow him then, too? Answer: No, for it is no one's duty to do wrong; we must obey God (who desires the right) rather than men [Acts 5:29]. What if the subjects do not know whether their prince is in the right or not? Answer: So long as they do not know, and cannot with all possible diligence find out, they may obey him without peril to their souls.

---

21   AE 45:114.

Here is no appeal to 'Quietism'—far from it. The citizen is bound to use "all possible diligence" to examine the morality of that which the authorities demand of him—and he is conscience-bound to disobey when that which is commanded is contrary to the Word of God. The Christian is not a passive 'subject' bound to robotically execute each and every command issued by civil authorities; rather, Christians are conscience-bound to examine every such demand, and to weigh the morality of that which is demanded by the civil authorities.

A recurrent theme for Luther in his writings on this broad topic is the inappropriateness of seeking a secular 'solution' to the 'religious' problems of his age—and vice versa. When the peasants sought to justify their rebellion against civil authority through appeals to the 'gospel' (e.g., the *Twelve Articles* [1525]), Luther turned his rage on them. Thus Luther declared in his *An Admonition to Peace* (1525), "The fact that the rulers are wicked and unjust does not excuse tumult and rebellion, for to punish wickedness does not belong to everybody, but to the worldly rulers who bear the sword. Thus Paul says in Romans xiii, and Peter in I Peter iii, that they are ordained of God for the punishment of the wicked."[22] And Luther's further comments made it clear that he understood that the peasants were being led by heretics who were confusing them concerning the very nature of the Gospel:

> See, dear friends, what kind of preachers you have and what they think of your souls. I fear that some prophets of murder have come among you, who would like, by your means, to become lords in the world, and do not care that they are endangering your life, property, honor, and soul, temporally and eternally. If, now, it is really your will to keep the divine law, as you boast, then do it. There it stands! God says, "Vengeance is mine; I will repay"; and again, "Be subject not only to good lords, but also to the wicked." If you do this, well and good; if not, you may, indeed, cause a calamity, but it will finally come upon yourselves.

22   Martin Luther, *Works of Martin Luther*, vol. IV (Philadelphia: Muhlenberg Press,) p. 227.

Heiko Oberman observed that Luther was utterly opposed to
the Joachimite fantasies of a 'New Age' which were common already in
the Reformation era, and have only become more widely adhered to in
the Modern Age. In Oberman's words: "Luther rejected all endeavors
to establish a kingdom of God on earth. ... Very much counter to the
temperament of his age—and of late, 'modern' times—Luther took a
vigorous stand against all efforts to wrest from God His timetable, and
to force—with sword in hand—the coming kingdom of peace."[23]

Luther's rhetoric took on a much darker cast when that which he
had maintained was only "idle chatter"—that is, violent revolution—ac-
tually came to pass. In *The Pursuit of the Millennium*, Norman Cohn notes
that "The causes of the German Peasants' War have been and no doubt
continue to be a subject of controversy... The well-being of the German
peasantry was greater than it had ever been; and particularly the peasants
who everywhere took the initiative in the insurrection, so far from being driven on by sheer misery and desperation, belonged to a rising and
self-confident class."[24] In point of fact, much of the initial tension was not
expressed in the form of insurrection; rather, it was "an intensification of the
tough, hardheaded bargaining which the peasantry had been conducting
for generations."[25] However, in Thuringia, Müntzer escalated the tensions
through his theologically-expressed call for a 'class struggle' against the nobility which left no room for peaceful settlement of the conflict.[26] Philip
of Hesse massed sufficient military force against the peasant forces in
Mühlhausen that their defeat seemed certain, thus, in Cohn's words:

---

23   Heiko A. Oberman, *Luther—Man between God and the Devil*, (New Haven
and London: Yale University Press, 1989), p. 62, 64.
24   (New York: Oxford University Press, 1970) p. 245.
25   ibid.
26   Thus, for example, in April 1525, Müntzer urged his supporters to slaugh-
ter their opponents: "At them, at them, while the fire is hot! Don't let your sword get
cold! ... So long as they are alive you will never shake off the fear of men. One can't
speak to you about God so long as they are reigning over you." (ibid., p. 248)

A battle fought under such circumstances could have only one possible result; but the princes nevertheless offered terms, promising the peasants their lives on condition that they handed over Müntzer and his immediate following. The offer was probably made in good faith, for in dealing with the insurrection in his own territories the Landgrave, while demanding submission, had also avoided unnecessary bloodshed. And the offer would probably have been accepted but for the intervention of Müntzer himself.[27]

The battle which ensued cost thousands of lives and led to recriminations which have reverberated down to this day, with Müntzer and his followers becoming the heroes of Marxist theoreticians, and the princes cast as brutal tyrants and Luther as the apologist for mindless butchery.

Thus far, we have examined Luther in his 'pre-confessional' period; that is, before the formal process of Reformation was begun through public acts such as the Saxon Visitation and its Articles, and the Augsburg Confession was presented to the diet in 1530. The developments which occurred politically in conjunction with the Diet of Augsburg led the secular rulers to demand that the jurists and theologians work together until they came to a common understanding. As Shoenberger observes, other Lutheran theologians such as Luther's bishop, Johannes Bugenhagen,[28] had already begun to build a case for resistance to the

---

27   ibid., p. 249–250.

28   "For example, Johannes Bugenhagen, a theologian close to Luther, answered in 1523 that a prince was required to protect his subjects against injustice from whatever source, just as he would protect them from robbery or murder. As servants of the law, possessors of the sword, and protectors of their people, the princes thus had the right to resist the Emperor. By 1529 Bugenhagen had organized his thoughts on this subject into a lengthy treatise which he presented to the Elector, thus confirming the fact that there was considerable support among the theological faculty for resistance; the arguments in it were built around two fundamentally Lutheran concepts, the notion of spheres of secular and spiritual authority and the duty of the prince or magistrate to protect his subjects." (Shoenberger, p. 7.)

18

authority of the Emperor. When rumors spread in 1528 of a coming attack by a league of Catholic leaders against the Lutheran territories, and when, in 1529, Emperor Charles V reneged on the agreement with the Lutheran princes which had been made at the Diet of Speyer in 1526, the secular authorities understood that further delay on a thorough examination of the theological and legal dimensions of the issue could not be tolerated. As Shoenberger notes:

> But while Luther refused his support, the jurists in the employ of the Elector were beginning to marshal legal arguments in support of resistance. In response to Philip of Hesse's continuing pleas, a great debate, carried on through formal communiqués and opinions, began among the lawyers and theologians attached to the courts and councils of the Protestant areas still in doubt over the justifiability of resistance to the Emperor; and out of this debate constitutional arguments for resistance began to be elaborated. These arguments, based upon a notion of the Empire as a limited monarchy, were an additional weapon for Philip of Hesse in his attempt to gain allies. He wrote, for example to the Margrave of Brandenburg-Ansbach ... that the relationship between the Emperor and the inferior magistrates, a category used to include both the princes and city governments who held Electoral status under the terms of the 1356 Golden Bull and those who did not, was a conditional one.[29]

When Elector John (1468–1532) inquired directly regarding the question "whether one can wage war for the sake of the Gospel in order to defend it with the sword," Bugenhagen's formal answer of September 1529 is quite illuminating, and is the position which Luther would later take up as his own. Bugenhagen readily conceded that in the normal course of events, citizens owed obedience to their secular lead-

29   Shoenberger, p. 8–9.

ers: "In his imperial role we intend to obey him in all matters, even more than others and in accordance with Christ's teaching, 'Render to Caesar what belongs to Caesar' [Matt. 22:21; Mark 12:17; Luke 20:25]."[30] However, this loyalty was vitiated when the rulers defied the Word of God and persecuted the Church: "'All authority is from God' [Rom. 13[:1]]. Therefore, when authority wishes to go against God or against God's word, then it ceases to have authority, as Samuel also says plainly to Saul in 1 Kings 15, 'Now, because you have rejected the LORD's word, He has also rejected you, so that you may not be king' [1 Kgs. 15[:23]]."[31] Bugenhagen explicitly declared that if the ruler becomes a persecutor, then the people have the right of resistance, citing, once again, the example of Saul: "However, if Saul had proceeded and had wished to compel the people with force from God's word to idolatry and had, to this end, begun to strike and to murder, I think that Samuel would have stabbed him mortally himself and would have joined the people in armed opposition to him."[32] For Bugenhagen, such argumentation was not a matter of abstract reflection on Old Testament history: he made the application to the direct circumstances confronting the Reformation in Germany.

VIII.

St. Paul says thereafter, "Whoever opposes authority opposes God's order" [Rom. 13:2]. God did not give anyone authority to suppress God's word or to rule over consciences. That is also not God's order but the devil's perversion. If one reads further in Paul one finds that this opinion is expressed clearly, namely, that God's authority is to protect, not to pervert, the godly and everything that is good [Rom. 13:3–6].

---

30   Johannes Bugenhagen, *Selected Writings*, trans. by Kurt K. Hendel, 2 vols., vol. 1, (Minneapolis: Fortress Press, 2015) p. 105.

31   ibid., p. 105–106.

32   ibid., p. 106.

IX.

Such authority is from God. We are obliged to respect it with our obedience and to contribute property, body, and life. Whoever opposes the authority earns his own condemnation. Those who desire to prevent it from having its authority, honor, and obedience are the people who oppose authority.

X.

However, when the authority itself transcends its authority ordained by God and asserts another authority to judge God's word and to oppress it, to compel people away from God, to rob, to murder, etc., to the eternal corruption of its people and its descendants, in that case one should acknowledge publicly that it acts unjustly. In such matters one has no command from God to obey. We also do not recognize it as our government and have also not sworn allegiance to it when it acts in such a way.[33]

In the months leading up to the Diet of Augsburg, Luther remained in agreement with those theologians who opposed armed resistance to Emperor Charles V. However, the breakthrough in his understanding came during the Torgau disputation later that year when jurists and theologians finally gathered to discuss the theological and legal issues pertaining to resistance to the Emperor:

The pressures upon Luther culminated in the calling of a public disputation at Torgau in October and November 1530. The Elector John intended thereby to force the Wittenberg theologians into an open confrontation with the Saxon jurists and thus to obtain a definitive resolution of his ethical and legal dilemma. The legal experts presented their position first, insisting that the Emperor was elected upon specific conditions

---

33   p. 106–107.

and was to rule in conjunction with the Estates. If he violated
the laws of the Empire, as he had done by proceeding against
the Protestants when their appeal to a Council was still pend-
ing, all their obligations to him were erased. ...

In the name of all the Wittenberg theologians, Luther presented a brief opinion admitting that, although they had always
preached nonresistance in the past, the theologians had not re-
alized that the constitution of the Empire in fact provided for
resistance under certain circumstances: "For when we previously taught, positively never to resist the established authority, we
did not know that such a right was granted by the laws of that
very authority, which we have at all times diligently instructed
people to obey." Thus the pastors with this brief declaration essentially passed the question of resistance to the jurists.[34]

In March 1531 the Smalcald League was formed as a means of defense
against the military forces of the Emperor. While Luther had hardly
become an advocate of armed resistance to tyranny, in his *Warning to
his Beloved Germans* (1531) Luther opened the door to armed resistance:

It is not becoming to me to counsel or incite war, but to preach
peace, which I have always been doing most ardently, as the
world must testify. ... But if it should come to war, I would not
have those who shall resist the murderous and bloodthirsty Papists censured as rebellious, but would have it called necessary
self-defense. ... A Christian knows well to render unto God the
things that are God's, and unto Caesar the things that are Caesar's, but not unto the bloodhounds that which is not theirs.
This will I say as a warning to my beloved Germans, that I
will not incite anyone to war, rebellion, or armed resistance, but
only to peace. But our devils, the Papists, will not have peace, ...
raving against the Holy Spirit, and insisting on war. I have not

34 Shoenberger, p. 10. Gritsch agrees with this assessment (p. 51).

done this, nor have I given cause to it, but they have so desired it. Their blood be upon their own head; I am not to blame and have most faithfully done my part. I will let Him judge who will, shall, and can judge. Unto Him be glory and honor, thanks and praise in eternity. Amen.[35]

This apologetic line would continue to be developed in Luther's private and public writings over the next decade—especially as the fear of war between the Emperor and the Smalcald League increased after 1536. Thus, for example, in a *Gutachten* for Elector John Frederick of Saxony and Landgrave Philip of Hesse, Luther, Justus Jonas, Martin Bucer, and Philip Melanchthon argued as follows concerning resistance to the Emperor:

> Every father is obliged, according to his ability, to protect his wife and children against outright murder, and there is no difference between a private murderer and the Emperor when he undertakes [to exercise] unjust force outside of his office, and especially, open or notorious unjust force. For open violence annuls all duty between subjects and superiors according to natural law.[36]

And Luther declared during an academic disputation in 1539:

> If one may resist the pope, one may also resist all those who defend and protect him. The pope seeks out the souls of all humanity, that is, he desires, above all, to subject each soul to his blasphemies, so that they go to hell for his sake. Hence it is necessary to march and rally against all the armies which fight under his command, *even though it means insurrection.* For we should not permit the damnation of souls ... If the emperor

---

35   quoted in Ernst August Brueggemann, *The Life of Dr. Martin Luther*, (St. Louis: Concordia Publishing House, 1904) p. 105.
36   quoted in Schoenberger, p. 16.

does not know where the church is — this can be tolerated. But if he wants to protect the werewolf [*Beerwolff*] — this cannot be tolerated. Instead, he must be opposed.[37]

However, already in the *Tischreden* of the early 1530s Luther was comparing the right of self-defense against common brigands to one's right to self-defense against unjust civil authorities:

> If, however, I caught someone, who was not exactly a tyrant, with my wife or daughter, so would I want to kill him. Likewise if he took by force from this one his wife, from another his daughter, from a third his fields and goods, and the citizens and subjects came together, and could no longer tolerate or endure his violence and tyranny; so could they kill him just as they would another murderer or robber on the street.[38]

After all, as Luther declared in April 1538: "This is not a theological matter but a legal one. If the Emperor undertakes war he will be a tyrant and will oppose our ministry and religion and then he will also oppose our civil and domestic life. Here there is no question whether it's permissible to fight for one's faith. On the contrary, it's necessary to fight for one's children and family."[39]

Finally, in April and May 1539, the leaders of the Smalcald League arranged a disputation: *Die zirkular disputation über das Recht des Widerstands gegen den Kaiser*, the theses of which are dated May 9, 1539. In these theses, Luther sets forth his doctrine of the three estates in the context of the Christian's life within the two kingdoms and establishes a definite contrast between that which must be sacrificed out of obedience to the first table of the Law, and that which must be defended un-

---

37   quoted in Gritsch, p. 51–52.
38   quote in Shoenberger, p. 17.
39   ibid., p. 18.

der the second table of the Law.[40] Early in the theses, Luther offers the following distinction:

> 22. For in the cause of the first table—buying and retaining those pearls of the kingdom of heaven—the field must be sold and all things must be left behind and lost.
>
> 23. For then what you justly have and own according to the second table of the Law for this life must be gladly lost for the sake of the first table, that is, for the sake of eternal life.
>
> 24. Outside the cause of the first table, that is, the confession, all things are to be obtained, preserved, defended, and administered.
>
> 25. For we are obliged by divine and natural law to obey the second table, that is, to maintain, nourish, protect and manage our body and this life.

The first table of the Law does not offer justification for defense of 'daily bread' and all first article blessings. Luther's point is that if it were solely a matter of persecution for the faith, then Christians should be willing to sacrifice all material goods to keep the faith. But such 'first table' concerns do not exist in isolation from the second table of the Law. And Luther invokes not only divine law, but natural law, to speak of the obligation to maintain and protect such first article gifts under the considerations of the second table of the Law. Thus, Luther declares in Theses 30: "Outside the cause of confession, the Christian is a citizen of this world and ought to do and to carry out those things which belong to his citizenship according to the second table." Therefore, this obligation carries certain responsibilities pertaining to self-defense, and the defense of family and possessions:

---

40   My thanks to Pastor Paul Rydecki for his assistance by quickly providing a preliminary translation of these theses. The original theses can be found in *W.A.* XXXIX, ii.

31. Now if a thief or a robber wants to harm you or rob from you because you are a Christian, you must resist the evil person, if you wish to be a godly citizen of this world,

32. For just as the magistrate himself resists him, whose member you are, so he commands you to resist him by virtue of the second table, which you are obliged to obey.

33. So if a thief wishes to kill you on a journey because of Christ, you should defend yourself, even if it means you have to kill the thief.

34. Since you know that the magistrate has prescribed that you are to resist thieves and to defend his citizens, in this very way you are obeying both the first and the second table.

35. Nor should it trouble you if he invokes Christ as an excuse, that is, the first table, since it is certain that he seeks to kill you, not because of Christ, but because of your property.

But what of the magistrate who becomes a thief? In Thesis 36, Luther maintains that if the magistrate "persecutes you on account of Christ, then all things are to be left behind, sold, and lost." But in Thesis 44, the contrast comes between "a magistrate who forbids evil"—whom we are obliged to obey—and, on the other hand, the injunction to "resist the evil man by virtue of the second table."

Following Luther's discussion of such principles, one comes to the heart of the matter: what is to be done concerning the Emperor and other civil authorities who afflict the faithful for the sake of the anti-christian pope? Luther clearly defines the fact that the papal office does not exist under any of the three estates. Rather he is "an adversary of God, a man of sin, a son of perdition," and, as Luther declares in Thesis 58: "Our Germans call it a *Beerwolf*, which the Greeks, if perhaps it had been known to them, would have been called ἀρκτόλυκον." Luther then offered a protracted analogy:

59. This animal is like a wolf, but, having been possessed by a demon, it tears everything apart and evades all hunting spears and weapons.

60. In order to defeat this creature, the whole countryside and all the towns, each and every man, have to attack together, and yet, even so, it still escapes their grasp.

61. Nor can anyone wait around here for the sentence of the judge or the decision of the council, for one must consider the imminent calamity and necessity.

62. If someone were to be wounded by this monster while hunting it to kill it, he would have no sense of guilt for having hunted it, but only for not having killed it.

63. Nor should anyone here be hindered by the fact that the judge or the peasant in the countryside may wish to set this animal free or even defend it.

64. For the judge and the peasant ought to know the nature of this monster and ought to hunt it even more vigorously than the hunters themselves.

65. If the judge and the peasants [who want to protect it] are killed by the hunters of this monster in the midst of all the confusion, no injustice will have befallen them.

66. Thus, if the pope were to instigate a war, he must be resisted like that furious and possessed monster, which is a real *Beerwolf*.

67. For he is neither a bishop nor a heretic nor a prince nor a tyrant, but the beast spoken of by Daniel who brings desolation to all things (Daniel 7:23, 11:36).

68. Nor should anyone be concerned that he has princes who fight for him, or kings or even the very Caesars, heralded with the title of "Church."

69. Whoever goes to war on behalf of a thief (whoever he may be), should expect the peril of war, with eternal damnation.

70. It saves neither kings nor princes nor even Caesars, the fact that they boast that they are defenders of the Church, since they are supposed to know what the Church is, [and what this *Beerwolf* is].

Thus, we get to the heart of the matter: the magistrate—even if he is Caesar—who goes to war for a thief "should expect the peril of war, with eternal damnation," while the one who fights against "kings or even the very Caesars" has nothing to fear from divine judgment, for, "If someone were to be wounded by this monster while hunting it to kill it, he would have no sense of guilt for having hunted it, but only for not having killed it"—even if he is 'only' a peasant. The reason is simple: the *Beerwolf* attacks the entire social order. Therefore, anyone who wages war on his behalf—regardless of their vocation—has stepped out of his office and is liable unto death. When rulers imperil the entire social order, they are no longer rulers, Luther argues, echoing Bugenhagen's argument of September 1529.

Such seeming insurrection is still reserved for circumstances in which the entire social order is at risk. Luther is never the rebel. But the position of the mature Luther became the bedrock for the entire doctrine of the Smalcald League. In Shoenberger's words:

> Moreover, Luther's pronouncements upon this issue were interpreted by Protestants in the years after his death as evidence that the initiator of the Reform had sanctioned resistance. In 1546, for example, his 1530 *Warnung an seine lieben Deutschen* was republished with a preface by Melanchthon; and it and the tract *Wider den Meuchler zu Dresden* were cited by the Lutherans who led the city of Magdeburg's famous year-long defiance of the Emperor in 1550. In addition, his 1539 letter to Lubeck of Cotbus and the "Etliche Schlüss-Reden" (the rel-

evant theses from the 1539 disputation) were both updated and republished as publicity for the Schmalkaldic League in 1547.[41]

Such an understanding of the invalidation of the authority of secular rulers was upheld in 1550, when the pastors of Magdeburg formally lent their support to the magistracy of the city resisting the power of the Emperor and those allied with him. In *A Confession of the Magdeburg Pastors Concerning Resistance to the Superior Magistrate*, the nine pastors of the city—led by Nicholas von Amsdorf—wrote as follows on April 13 of that year:

> The powers that be are ordained of God to protect the good and punish the bad (Romans 13), but if they start to persecute the good, they are no longer ordained of God.
>
> There are to be sure degrees of tyranny and if a magistrate makes unjust war upon his subjects contrary to his plighted oath, they may resist, though they are not commanded to do so by God.
>
> But if a ruler is so demented as to attack God, then he is the very devil who employs mighty potentates in Church and State. When, for example, a prince or an emperor tampers with marriage against the dictates of natural law, then in the name of natural law and Scripture he may be resisted.[42]

The realities of the Smalcald War brought a number of the points enumerated by Luther in 1539 (and earlier) into clear focus. In Friedeburg's words, "the Lutherans and other Protestants had learned from the lesson of Elector Moritz of Saxony and from the crisis of the Interim that often there was no godly prince in sight to protect the faithful against

41   Shoenberger, p. 19.
42   quote in *Christianity and Revolution—Radical Christian Testimonies (1520–1650)*, ed. by Lowell H. Zuck, (Philadelphia: Temple University Press, 1975) p. 137–138.

the persecutors."[43] The Calvinist Johannes Althusius (1563–1638) "argued that the law of nature permitted a body politic, that is, a people under the rule of law, to defend itself against unwarranted attacks."[44] Among those who found Althusius' arguments to be persuasive was Johann Gerhard:

> Gerhard places the well-being of the fatherland clearly above the tyrant. Quoting much of the argument of the 1530s to 1550, which he had from Friedrich Hortleder's recent publication of 1618, Gerhard reminds the reader that a tyrant loses his title as magistrate, and that self-defense against such a tyrant, in effect a private person, was a right by law of nature. Like König and Althusius, Gerhard shifted the locus of duty to defend the laws against a tyrant from the imperial princes to the body politic and those who love it. Like Selinus, Althusius, and König, he declines to pinpoint a specific group within a given territory which might exercise such self-defense. Yet the magistrate who breaks the laws of the body politic becomes a tyrant. He destroys the bonds of obedience that binds subjects to their true magistrate. And although Gerhard declines to be more explicit, he insists that the prince as magistrate remains below the commonwealth for which he serves, and that the well-being of the fatherland was more important than the insane desires of a single person. The defense against a tyrant is allowed by law of nature.[45]

---

43   Robert V. Friedeburg, "In Defense of Patria: Resisting Magistrates and the Duties of Patriots in the Empire from the 1530s to the 1640s," in *The Sixteenth Century Journal* 32:2 (Summer 2001) p. 370.

44   ibid., p. 371.

45   ibid., p. 372.

Pietism and the Submission of the Church to the State

Given the confessional Lutheran commitment to such a clear un-derstanding of the character of the true magistrate, how did the Lutheran Church come to be burdened by a submissive attitude toward political absolutism? In no small part because of the machinations of the Pietists, who used the power of the State to break the authority of the confessional Lutheran Church. As Gawthrop observes in *Pietism and the Making of Eighteenth-Century Prussia*, "during the confessional period the Lutheran Church, even in theory, never understood its role as one of subservience to the state."[46] The growth of the power of the State over against the Church was connected with rise of the Pietists: Pietist the-ology was of use to the aims of the secular authorities. In Gawthrop's assessment:

> ...it was only at the very end of the seventeenth century, within the Lutheran Pietist movement, that there emerged the kind of fully Promethean spirituality capable of contributing so substantially to the bureaucratization of post-1713 Prussia. What emerged, in other words, was a Christianity that, upon repudiating the values associated with the traditional metaphysical order, redefined the religious quest as primarily an endeavor in which all spiritual, social, and natural resources must be utilized for the self-conscious build-up of human power.[47]

Thus, for example, Pietism's confessional indifference played to the immigration schemes by the authorities of the ruling class:

---

46   Richard L. Gawthrop, *Pietism and the Making of Eighteenth-Century Prussia*, (Cambridge: Cambridge University Press, 1993) p. 101–102.
47   ibid., p. 87.

In the eyes of such princes, Pietism constituted a faction within the Lutheran church that, unlike the orthodox majority, was not opposed to the immigration of non-Lutheran refugees—an important source of capital and skills for the impoverished German polities. Though actual sympathy for Pietism did not run very deep at the worldly courts, such pragmatic considerations helped soften otherwise hostile perceptions on the part of many of the courtiers.[48]

It is the "Promethean" character of later Pietism which is of particular interest to Gawthrop in his analysis of Pietism's contribution to the centralization of political power in Prussia. More specifically, it was the emphasis by August Hermann Francke and Halle Pietism on the reform of outward behavior that was brought into the service of Prussian absolutism: "Spener believed that reform of the Lutheran church would, eventually and in some unspecified way, bring about the desired change in society. The more radical Francke worked for the simultaneous transformation of both the church and the social order."[49] According to Gawthrop, Francke refocused Pietism on a very specific agenda of outward reform because of his own inner spiritual confusion, and thus his 'conversion experience,' rather than granting him spiritual peace, "… seems to have initiated, instead, a valiant, grandiose, and perhaps ultimately futile attempt to escape his own sense of emptiness and vulnerability. … Francke's was a truly Promethean spirituality, an obsession with power, action, and domination, fueled by the vision of an infinite challenge to be faced."[50] For Frederick William I (1688–1740), the Halle Pietism was a perfect reinforcement for his personal ideology in which "this self-centered, autocratic king justified the demands he placed on them on the grounds that to serve the Prussian state was to further God's work in the world. … With respect to the original germination of

---

48   ibid., p. 115.
49   ibid., p. 150.
50   ibid., p. 148–149.

the Prussian political culture and the eighteenth-century Prussian state system, then, the Protestant Prometheanism of Frederick William I and Halle Pietism played a decisive, energizing role."[51]

Ideologists such as Christian Thomasius (1655–1728) engaged in an active campaign to strip the Church of its God-given authority and to subject it to the whims of secular powers. As a political philosopher and one of the founding figures at Halle, Thomasius played a leading role in the "philosophical, theological, and jurisprudential conflicts" between Pietist Halle and the confessional Lutherans of Leipzig. For Thomasius, "The church is in the state, and the state is not in the church"[52] and "he was engaged in vehement disputation with the clerical, philosophical and juridical defenders of the early modern confessional state."[53] Thomasius' promulgation of his views had led to his being banned from lecturing in Dresden, and thus he fled to Brandenburg in 1690 to help found the University of Halle. Hunter is overt regarding the purpose for Halle's existence being opposition to confessional Lutheran theology and practice: "Halle was designed to weaken the grip of Lutheran orthodoxy through the pre-eminence of its secularist law faculty and the staffing of its theology faculty with anti-orthodox Lutheran Pietists ... Thomasius ... provided the court with a style of political jurisprudence sympathetic to the establishment of princely territorial supremacy".[54] Thus, for example, Thomasius denied to the clergy even the authority to determine that the doctrines proclaimed by a false teacher are heretical; rather, such authority resided with the State. If pastors insisted on labeling a false teacher as a "heretic," then the State should suppress the orthodox teacher: "This the magistrate should not tolerate, advising them that according to holy scripture one should avoid

---

51   ibid., p. 271, 273.
52   quoted in Ian Hunter, *The Secularlisation of the Confessional State—The Political Thought of Christian Thomasius*, (Cambridge: Cambridge University Press, 2007) p. 2.
53   ibid., p. 4.
54   ibid, p. 10.

a heretic but not persecute him. And if they do not want to accept this advice, then he should punish them as disobedient and as rebels."[55]

When Frederick II (1712–1786) became king of Prussia after the death of his father, Pietism had largely completed its transformation into Rationalism—at least within the heart of the autocrat. But the social-reformation orientation of Halle Pietism had conditioned many among the ranks of the Prussian clergy to continue serving as instruments of the king of Prussia:

> Their duties as local field agents of the government included such tasks as planting trees, announcing royal decrees from the pulpit, teaching peasants how to cultivate the soil, and providing the public authorities with population statistics and information on weather conditions, crops, and floods. Under Frederick William I and Frederick II the Protestant clergy was, in principle, completely subordinate to the personal will of these vigilant sovereigns. Written instructions to the Consistories regulated every aspect of the clerical office.[56]

Later abominations such as the *Deutsche Christen* movement, which perverted Christian teaching and practice in service of the Nazi regime, were simply further applications of a perverted notion which entered during the Pietistic period. The advocates of political quietism do not have Luther for their theological inspiration; rather, their doctrine has its origins in the efforts by the theological descendants of Pietists and Rationalists to appropriate decontextualized Luther citations for the purpose of serving Leviathan.

---

55   quoted in Hunter, p. 23.
56   Robert M. Bigler, *The Politics of German Protestantism*, (Berkeley: University of California Press, 1972) p. 8.

The American Republic

A mong the Reformation-era jurists who aided the work of the Lutheran Reformation, few could be held in higher regard than the founder of the Marburg school, Johannes Eisermann (1485–1558). As Witte observes, the Marburg school was particularly influential in the application of Lutheran theology to the law: "Like their Wittenberg colleagues, these Marburg jurists built on Luther's theology, particularly as distilled in his two-kingdoms framework. But they gave new legal prominence to Luther's theories of the priesthood of all believers, the Christian vocation, and the role of Christian conscience in decision-making."[57] The contribution of the jurists has been noted previously, but for this context we include a brief application from the thought of Eisermann to the second portion of our consideration. Witte drew three lessons pertaining to the "story of the birth and growth of the commonwealth tradition" in the thought of Eisermann:

> One lesson is that we Christians today can and must learn from the experiences of prior civilizations. A modern Christian theorist would do especially well to absorb the social, legal, and political instruction of the advanced civilizations of Greece and Rome, both before and after the coming of Christ. Following humanist conventions of his day, Eisermann took this maxim to heart, peppering his tracts with all manner of spicy references to Plato, Aristotle, Cicero, Seneca, and various early Roman jurists. ...
>
> A second lesson of this history is that there is no single foreordained or natural system of society, politics, and law. Every people chooses its own social form, its own political

structure, and its own system of law based on a "combination of nature, custom, and reason." ...

A third lesson of this history is that there is no single person – far less a single dynasty – in a commonwealth that naturally should rule. ... The choice of leadership in a commonwealth should turn upon a person's virtue and wisdom, not upon his connections or bloodline. Eisermann did not develop this point into a more general theory of popular sovereignty, as later Protestant theorists would do. But he did advert several times to the importance of periodic elections of officials as a means to ensure rule by the best rather than by the best connected.[58]

Eisermann's understanding of the origins of the commonwealth, in combination with the careful historical scholarship of the Marburg school, offers relatively easy comparison with the quintessential Republic of the Modern Age: the American Republic inextricably linked with its 1787–1789 Federalist constitution.

Despite the crudely reductionist assumptions of modern day advocates and opponents of the constitution which was written in the generation of the War of Independence, a profoundly complex intellectual landscape existed at the time of the nation's founding which resists many of the attempts to boil down the thought of the founders to a few pithy observations. There was an awareness in the founding generation of the particularity of that which was being undertaken, in the sense that there was a knowledge of classical antiquity and the history of political philosophy which is essentially unrivaled today. As Russell Kirk observed:

Study of Greek and Latin literature, and of the ancient world's history and politics, loomed much larger in American education during the latter half of the eighteenth century than

---

58   ibid., p. 146–147..

36

it does in American education today. ... But from such study the American leaders of the War of Independence and the constitution-making era learned, by their own account chiefly what political blunders of ancient times ought to be avoided by the Republic of the United States. ...

Leading Americans did study closely the old Greek constitutions. In his *Defence of the Constitutions of Government of the United States of America* (published in 1787, on the eve of America's Great Convention), John Adams examines critically twelve ancient democratic republics, three ancient aristocratic republics, and three ancient monarchial republics—and finds them all inferior to the political system of the new Republic of the United States. Alexander Hamilton, James Madison, and John Jay, the authors of the *Federalist Papers*, often referred to "the turbulent democracies of ancient Greece" (Madison's phrase) and to other ancient constitutions. In general, those three American statesmen found the political systems of Greece and Rome "as unfit for imitation, as they are repugnant to the genius of America" (again, Madison's phrase).[59]

The force of such influences on the political thought of the founding generation was not spent until at least the passing of the last major figure of that age, James Monroe, whose posthumously-published work, *The People, The Sovereigns*, offered an analysis of ancient forms of government as a means of better understanding the needs of the republic in our own age.

A critical distinction between sovereignty and governance lay at the root of the genius of the American Republic. Thus, for example, James Madison declared on August 31, 1787 during the Constitutional Convention, as the delegates discussed the authority of

---

59   Russell Kirk, *America's British Culture*, (New Brunswick and London: Transaction Publishers, 1993) p. 98.

future conventions: "The people were in fact, the fountain of all power, and by resorting to them, all difficulties were got over. They could alter constitutions as they pleased. It was a principle in the Bills of rights, that first principles might be resorted to."[60] This point was also expressly made in the public apologetic which was made for the constitution by way of that series of essays which is now known as the *Federalist Papers*, when Madison wrote:

> As the people are the only legitimate fountain of power, and it is from them that the constitutional charter, under which the several branches of government hold their power, is derived; it seems strictly consonant to the republican theory, to recur to the same original authority, not only whenever it is necessary to enlarge, diminish, or new model the powers of government; but also whenever any one of the departments may commit encroachments on the chartered authorities of the others.[61]

The understanding at work in the constitution is a division between *sovereignty* and *governance*. Thus, although those of 'democratic' propensities might imagine their favored doctrines siren sounds in the language of Madison, the reality is something far different (as is demonstrated by Federalist No. 10 in its vehement denunciation of democracy). Or, in the words of James Monroe:

> When it is known that the government of an individual, in which the people have no participation, is despotic, it might be inferred that that which passed to the opposite extreme, in which the whole power was vest in, and exercise by, the people collectively, was the most free and the best that human wisdom could devise. If men were angels, that result would follow, but in that case, there would be no necessity for any government. It

---

60   *Documentary History of the Constitution*, (Washington: Department of State, 1900) volume 3, p. 656.
61   Federalist No. 49, p. 255.

is the knowledge that all men have weaknesses, and that many have vices, that makes government necessary; and in adopting one, it is the interest of all that it should be formed in such manner as to protect the rights and promote the happiness of the whole community.[62]

The founders reject collapsing sovereignty and governance into the hands of a single group of people; just as the three branches of government developed a tension between those charged with governance, so the division between sovereigns and government was intended as a check on tyrannical developments. As Monroe wrote:

> The terms Sovereignty and Government have generally been considered as synonymous. Most writers on the subject have used them in that sense. To us, however, they convey very different ideas, as they must to all who analyze the subject on principle. The powers may be separated and placed in distinct hands, and it is the faculty of making that separation, which is enjoyed by one class of governments alone, which secures to it many of the advantages which it holds over all others. The separation may take place in the class in which the sovereign power is vested in the people. It cannot in that in which it is vested in an individual, or a few, nor can it in that which is mixed, or compounded of the two principles.[63]

Those charged with the authority of governance are ultimately accountable to those who possess the sovereignty; thus, within the constitutional limits prescribed to them, the governing authorities exercise their responsibility, but such power as has been addressed to them is not absolute:

---

62   James Monroe, *The People, the Sovereigns, being a Comparison of the Government of the United States with those of the Republics which have Existed Before, with the Causes of their Decadence and Fall*, introduction by Russell Kirk (Cumberland, Virginia: James River Press, 1987), p. 11.

63   Monroe, *The People, the Sovereigns*, p. 7.

In governments founded on the sovereignty of the people, in which the two powers are separated from each other, there is a reciprocal action of the government on the people, and of the people on the government, which is unceasing. The people prescribe the rule by compact by which they shall be governed, and in so doing they prescribe the functions and duties of the governing power, which acts on them individually and equally. They prescribe also, in the same instrument, the manner in which their own power in the capacity of sovereign shall be exercised. Each party has its duties to perform, on the faithful performance of which the success of the system depends. ... The government must be competent to its objects, and enjoy a freedom of action in the discharge of its duties, within the sphere prescribed, and on the principles of the compact. Misconduct and delinquency in those who administer it should be punishable and be punished, in the mode provided for by the system and executed under it. As the power proceeds from the people, it must be made subservient to their purposes, and this cannot be accomplished, unless those who exercise it feel their responsibility to their constituents in every measure which they adopt, and look to the people and not to themselves.[64]

Much has been made in recent years of the so-called "lesser magistracy" and its role in resisting tyranny.[65] Thus, for example, during the Seige of Magdeburg (1550–1551), the Lutheran pastors of that city "took for granted the right of the lesser magistrates to resist."[66] Circumstances such as those which befell the citizens of Magdeburg took place under

---

64 Monroe, *The People, the Sovereigns*, p. 9.
65 See, for example: David Mark Whitford, *Tyranny and Resistance—The Magdeburg Confession and the Lutheran Tradition* (St. Louis: Concordia Publishing House, 2001) and Matthew J. Trewhella, *The Doctrine of the Lesser Magistrates* (self-published by the author, 2013).
66 Whitford, p. 78.

a theory of government which located sovereignty in the magistracy. A very different understanding is at work in the American Republic. Under law, those who hold the sovereignty established the character of governing authority.

> It is only in governments in which the people possess the sovereignty that the two powers can be placed in distinct bodies; nor can they in them otherwise than by the institution of a government by compact, to which all the people are parties, and in which those who fill its various departments and offices are made their representatives and servants. In those instances the sovereignty is distinct from the government, because the people who hold the one are distinct from their representatives who hold and perform the duties of the other. One is the power which creates; the other is the subject which is created. One is always the same; the other may be modified at the will of those who made it. Thus the Constitution becomes the paramount law, and every act of the government, and of every department in it, repugnant thereto, void.[67]

Much is made these days of the so-called "general welfare" clause of the Preamble to the Constitution as authorizing a broad range of governmental action, but the irony in all of this attention is that it neglects the entire purpose of the Preamble, which is a statement of the principle of sovereignty enunciated by Madison and Monroe: "We the People of the United States... do ordain and establish this Constitution for the United States of America." The intention of the Constitution was that those who held the sovereignty were expressing the nature of the governmental authority which they established, and delineating the clear boundaries of that authority.

In the arrangement of the departments of the government, and distribution of their powers, great care should be

---

67   Monroe, *The People, the Sovereigns*, p. 8.

taken. It must be divided into three branches: legislative, executive and judicial, and each endowed with appropriate powers and made independent of the other. Liberty cannot exist if adequate provision be not made for this great object. The other instances in which the people may exercise their sovereign power relate to the compact itself. If defects are seen in it, they have a right to amend it, and to correct them according to their best judgment, and at pleasure. … If in the case of amendments, the agency of the government is admitted in any form, it must be in the mode prescribed by the existing Constitution, and in which it will act merely as the instrument of the people in their character as the sovereign power of the state.

The separation, however, of the sovereignty from the government, when the people possess the sovereignty, depends altogether on their will. They must be united in their hands, in like manner as in the other classes.[68]

This understanding of sovereignty and governmental authority was long upheld by students of the constitution. As a case in point, one may consider Thomas Cooley's (1824–1898) oft-cited work, *A Treatise on the Constitutional Limitations which rest upon the Legislative Power of the States of the American Union*, which was first published in 1868 and which went through six editions by 1890. Cooley defined sovereignty as follows: "*Sovereignty*, as applied to States, imports the supreme, absolute, uncontrollable power by which any State is governed. A State is called a sovereign State when this supreme power resides within itself, whether resting in a single individual, or in a number of individuals, or in the whole body of the people."[69] Cooley clearly enunciated the particular character of the American Republic: "The theory of our political system

68   Monroe, *The People, the Sovereigns*, p. 10.

69   Thomas M. Cooley and Victor H. Lane, *A Treatise on the Constitutional Limitations which rest upon the Legislative Power of the States of the American Union*, 7th edition, (Boston: Little, Brown, and Company, 1903) p. 3.

is that the ultimate sovereignty is in the people, from whom springs all legitimate authority."[70] Within this republic, then, the governing authority established by the sovereigns is expressed in the law of the constitution:

> But the term *constitutional government* is applied only to those whose fundamental rules or maxims not only locate the sovereign power in individuals or bodies designated or chosen in some prescribed manner, but also define the limits of its exercise so as to protect individual rights, and shield them against the assumption of arbitrary power. ...
>
> In American constitutional law, the word *constitution* is used in a restricted sense, as implying the written instrument agreed upon by the people of the Union, or of any one of the States, as the absolute rule of action and decision for all departments and officers of the government, in respect to all the points covered by it, which must control until it shall be changed by the authority which established it, and in opposition to which any act or regulation of any such department or officer, or even the people themselves, will be altogether void.[71]

Sovereignty was, for Cooley, something which found practical expression the body of those who possess the franchise: "As a practical fact the sovereignty is vested in those persons who are permitted by the constitution of the State to exercise the elective franchise."[72] But in this exercise of sovereignty, a clear distinction between sovereigns and governmental authority must be maintained. In Monroe's words:

> The two great principles must, therefore, be considered fundamental and invariable, in regard to government, in which the people hold the sovereignty—first, that the government be separated from the sovereignty; the second, that it be divided

---

70   Cooley and Lane, p. 56.
71   Cooley and Lane, p. 5.
72   Cooley and Lane, p. 57.

into three separate branches, legislative, executive, and judicial, and that each be endowed with its appropriate powers, and be made independent of the others. It is by a faithful observance of these principles, and a wise execution of them, that tyranny may be prevented; the government be made efficient for all its purposes; and the power of the people be preserved over it, in all its operations. Unite the government with the sovereignty, although it be in the people, and every species of abuse, with the certain overthrow of both, will follow. Concentrate all power in one body, although it be representative, and the result, if not so prompt, will, nevertheless, be equally fatal.[73]

The division of sovereignty and governmental authority expresses a situation which is radically different from that which existed in any former model generally known in the realm of political philosophy, and it is an understanding with profound theological significance. The constitution is predicated on the understanding that not the elected representatives, but rather the body politic, is sovereign, and constitutes the higher authority. That point which Luther and his noble coadjutors (and those later theologians such as Johann Gerhard) expressed—that is, that a tyrant lost his divinely-bestowed authority when he became a tyrant persecuting the Church or violating the tenets of natural law—is all the more applicable in a circumstance in which sovereignty is explicitly separated from governance. That which was confessed by the clergy of Magdeburg—"The powers that be are ordained of God to protect the good and punish the bad (Romans 13), but if they start to persecute the good, they are no longer ordained of God."—has application when the will of the sovereigns, expressed in a law, is willfully disregarded. If even in a circumstance where governance and sovereignty are held by the same individuals, classes, or parties, still the authority of governance is vitiated in cases of tyranny, how much more so when those who administer the State are subordinate to a sovereignty which is retained by

73   Monroe, *The People, the Sovereigns*, p. 13.

the people? Far from encouraging political quietism in such a circumstance, a consistent confessional Lutheran theology of the relationship between Church and State requires Christians to clearly uphold those principles which the Lutheran fathers enunciated when confronted by the tyranny of Emperor Charles V. Tyrants deny that they are answerable either to God or man. For those who believe God's Word, it is necessary to place one's reliance on the Word, and call upon such tyrants to repent. The tyrant who despises the divine Word and spurns the rule of law will likely care little for such calls to repentance, but the Church will have discharged her duty.

While enduring house arrest in the latter days of the Second World War, Norwegian Lutheran Bishop Eivind Berggrav wrote a powerful work *Staten og mennesket* (*Man and State*), which is worthy of careful study. On this occasion, one quote must suffice:

> What we need is not more "national power" but more law: not an increase of the right to use force, but a deeper respect for the law as something transcendent. We need not more bravado, but more reverence. The tragedy of the present situation lies in the fact that *by its self-exaltation the state undermines its very existence.* It abandons the moral law and lands in the clutches of the law of the jungle: every man for himself. The modern state is in process of organizing the whole of society on the the basis of a state of internal war. ...
>
> To put the whole matter briefly: *The modern state is a power, which, if it does not become human, inevitably becomes demonic.* The modern state is beset on every hand by tragedy.[74]

---

[74]   p. 42.